STORM
OVER
HACKENSACK

STORM OVER HACKENSACK

AUGUST KLEINZAHLER

MOYER BELL LIMITED   MT. KISCO, NY

Acknowledgements

Some of these poems first appeared in the following magazines:
Art International/The Lugano Review, Brick, The Cimarron Review, Credences, Epoch, The Fiddlehead, Four by Four, Giants Play Well in the Drizzle, The Grosseteste Review, Harper's, The Kenyon Review, The LA Weekly, Montemora, Ninth Decade, Occident, Origin, Prism International, Queen's Quarterly, Scripsi, Sulfur, The Threepenny Review, Writing.

Incident in Chinatown was issued as a broadside by the New Jersey State Council of the Arts in conjunction with the Rutgers University Art Department.

Sundown at Fletcher's Field appeared as one of two poems in a broadside issued by **The Word Bookstore** in Montreal.

Ahasuerus appeared as a broadside issued by **Barbarian Press** in Mission, British Columbia.

A BL&T With Old Ed Hopper appeared in **Edward Hopper: Development of an American Artist,** published by the Art Museum of South Texas in conjunction with an exhibit organized by the Whitney Museum.

Lightning Bugs appeared as a poster on the municipal bus systems of New York City, Washington, D.C., Chicago, Los Angeles and San Francisco, courtesy of Winston Network, Inc., as part of **Streetfare Journal: The Magazine of the Rider.**

A number of the poems included in this collection previously appeared in **The Sausage Master of Minsk,** Villeneuve, Montreal, 1977; **A Calendar of Airs,** The Coach House Press, Toronto, 1978; a pamphlet, **The Haight,** Northern Lights, London, 1984; and a booklet, **Dainties & Viands,** Galloping Dog, Newcastle, 1985.

The author wishes to acknowledge the generous assistance of the General Electric Foundation, The New Jersey State Council on the Arts, the Ontario Arts Council, The Canada Council on the Arts, the Montemora Foundation and the Djerassi Foundation.

Library of Congress Cataloging in Publication Data

Kleinzahler, August.
    Storm over Hackensack.

    I. Title.
PR9199.3.K482S7 1985   811'.54   85-9061
ISBN 0-918825-06-7
ISBN 0-918825-08-3 (pbk.)

In memory of my brother, Harris

Stolen away by merciless fortune
my brother

So accept these gifts in our parents' custom
offered in grief to the shades below
darling brother
> through a brother's tears
> forever
>> —Hail & Farewell.

Catullus

Table of Contents

A CALENDAR OF AIRS

WHERE SOULS GO

Where Souls Go

No telling where: down the hill
and out of sight—
soapbox derby heroes in a new dimension.
Don't bother to resurrect them
unless some old newsreel clip
catches them shocked
with a butterknife in the toaster.
Countless snaps and episodes in space,
once you hit the viewfinder that fits.
It's a lie anyway, all Hollywood—
the Mind is a too much thing
cleansing itself like a great salt sea.
Rather, imagine them in the eaves

among pigeons
or clustered 'round the D-Train's fan
as we cross the bridge to Brooklyn.
And make that a Friday night
July say. We are walking past
the liquor store to visit our love.
Two black boys are eating Corn Doodles
in the most flamboyant manner possible.
She waits, trying
to have the best song on as we arrive.
The moon is blurred.
Our helicopters are shooting at fieldworkers.
The Mets are down 3–1 in the 6th.

16

The creases in the schoolboy's pegged wool slacks
blow flat against his ankles
as he puffs uphill in the Bronx. The day is
raw and new. He didn't do his Latin.

Below and to the east smoke braids
and drifts further east. Levering and stoking
out there grown men in coveralls slog through
the dead hours, while in their lunchpails

bologna sweats. A bird is in the schoolboy's head:
Shelley's skylark. Ha, that prink
never lurched uptown on the El with squads
of plump domestics lost in romance comics

and down each night
past the Italian cookie factory, its sigh-
fetching smells. Life
is a tunnel the kid's soul spills out of—

blithe crystal missile
kissing down in a meadow, high
over the Bay of Naples.
Girls are there

in bright cotton dresses pulled just past
the knee. In gestures ritual,
tacit and wild,
they offer him glances, then sweet things to eat.

This is the place our friend shall run
the circuit of every glad thing, flare
and perish
          exquisitely.

November in West New York

Roofer looks out on the street
flipping his knife
how the Cuban salesman showed him.
You just press the release
and snap your wrist.
Here, try it.
No, not like that, like this.

The street's three maples
are nearly stripped
of the yellow flecking tenement brick
but no storm yet.
Just a soft slow afternoon
on 52nd street.

He's waiting on the storm
and two fat bids.
—One good fucking storm
with lots of wind.
And hail.
And destruction, he says

flipping that blade,
waiting for the phone to ring.

Coconut Oil

Cool wind, a wind
        in advance of milder fronts
        pulls maple limbs
into sluggish approbation of any air at all
even air laced with car exhaust
and copra
        refined nearby into soap
the willowy pale daughters of Indiana make
top wage under kleig lights
drawing languidly along their arms.

And the old woman with swollen legs
pulls a hanky from her bag
           wiping away the film
of grit and sweat
that's settled on her face.
With this breeze the next block won't be
half so difficult.
        She is on her way to the market
in order to buy
a nice piece of fish and some soap.

Hot Night on East 4th

A shriek hits the membrane
that canopies the street,
falls, and the trough gets it.
Sediment thickens with it,
those glittery spores
that took their shot and fell.

The monster stirs
under this midden of filth
we love on, chafing
himself against the crust
too miserable to rage.

Cat jism, perfume—
the radio horn man blows
his hole through
again blows, again with spite
again
till no more horn
none.

Vancouver

Downstairs, Sal, of Sal's Paradise Club
stirs a fizz drink for a mummy blond.
—*Thanks, Sal.*
Black filthy rain it's raining
like a grudge is out
but the neon mermaid over the fish place
looks best that way, in the rain.

Freighters queue in the bay,
1 2   34   5
waiting to dock.
A sailor aboard the lead ship, a Dane
sniffs saltchuck and lights himself a smoke.
He gazes out to the shimmering downtown spit.
He likes how tobacco and saltsea mix in his nose.

Relaxing in California

They are coming out, emptying
into the plaza of concrete and fronds—
food handlers, clerks
going home.
        The sky is blue, skyblue; blue
buses line up at the curb.
We are on our way home
before the sun gets lost in the western sea.

To the hills threaded with gold
we go.

        Down sidewalks, under sills
where music hangs down
by no thread at all,
home.

        To our shaded valleys
where fugue after fugue dissolves in the loam.

Downtown,
        where little boys play at rocks
        and chophouses smoke.

Along this pivot's luscious course
sky turns the blue
Mommy's Chevy was

and t.v. sets go *pock pock pong*
under the clear crisp sickle moon.

Boys' Night Out

Of an evening in spring
early spring
after the winds have died down
it's good to go off with a friend

and drink
ride down boulevards
to the sea and back
drinking

gabbling about women and books
catalpa in bloom
dog with a pizza crust hanging
out its jaw

and drink
because wine makes lords of men
because too many homilies seem true
and that must be fixed

and when you're out of jack
words
beat at the knees
your belly full

go home
open the bedroom window and spew
right at the stars
spew

till you're clean
of the bile and phlegm
all the poisons making a stew
here they come

along with hatefulness
and grief
the *I'm sorry sorry*
out with that too

yard cat's freaked
and the air is cool
goes deep down
new

Autumn in the Western Hills

When storms assail the summer palace
driving deer under canopies of brake,
pine boughs take on new life in wind
as the old courtesan, juggler and cook
keep close 'round the flame
sipping the stew's dark broth,
emptying what few jars of wine remain.

They'd travel days for the sunsets:
dignitaries, their pinch-toed consorts.
And after the sun,
when puma range down from the hills for deer,
night-tinted smoke flooding the valleys—
a dream,
the tiger lily composted.

One moon ago, coolness at evening:
a delicate astringent;
now, sunflower stalks routed to earth,
the passes treacherous.
So they sit, nursing the fire,
little else but to get stiff and listen
between gusts and pellets of rain

for word from the Capital.

By the Tagus

With fond Jean in the pastelaria at closing
coffee ends
                as did the Roman, Visigoth & Moor
in a weird apse
bastard tile

            A white peacock screams
from the castle above
then tears the night apart once more

                    Love   Love

How it scalds the rainbow pheasant
        ibex   dove   flamingo

                            Love

in the castle garden

                            Love

in a searing cry

dragging its spur through the harbor night

                    then gone
in a suturing breeze

Indian Summer Night: The Haight

The 43 bus at Carl&Cole
steps on the comic's line
but applause and laughter
waft up the lane.
           A *ranger* on the grass
bestirs himself,
spooked

then barks back a laugh of his own,
an unwholesome laugh,
stiffening the neighbor cats.

The summer my sister worked at Palisades Park
I'd stay awake till midnight,
listening.
When the breeze in the maples was right
you could hear her

my sister,
over the loudspeaker a quarter mile away
telling barkers patrons and freaks,
everybody,
the last voice before the lights went out,

—*Thank you. Good night.*

Hamburger

They come to resemble Buddhas,
these old fucks,
with their *hamburgeronly15¢/lb.*
andgoodmeat,too.

They're out there on the street
like undercover cops,
short-brim and necktie,
watching it all go to hell.

                Vestigial,
dead in the pants . . .

—*Miami before the war,*
you should have seen it:
paradise.

       A lemon tree in every yard.

Real Hair

How come all youze got fairy hair
cuts cost 10 bucks wid bangs
Dey don' e'en shave ya neck
mudge less clip yaw nozdrils

I oughta cha'ge a sawbuck,
wea' high heel shoes
      like some jigaboo

Shame,

shame on a nice fella like you

With Jasmine in Bloom

Her spirit wouldn't stray this far—
not like my brother,
the electric of him yanking me up.
Chicago she liked well enough,
but the coast . . .
not Utah *and* the Rockies.

Swollen, waxen, blanketed in cats,
smoking unfiltereds,
making cracks . . .
                    Her ghost
brushes past them,
in the kitchen, near dawn—
a breath along the nerves' boundary.

Summers were hard on her anyhow.

EVENING, IN
A-MINOR

Rezoned

Ten mighty condos suck
amperes
     under pink night sky, stars
     little jets transect
& moon
     so gala other years no
     big wheel.

Pyknic, bejeweled
the widows gather
where there was once a wood my brother hid in
rested himself
     against a birch, gazing
at Harlem, its
hills
     muffled on the river's far shore.

This place, here
my brother came
     to nurse on the stillness,
     the changing light
          until somewhere near
a branch cracking
     set off a hubbub of frightened starlings.

Evening, Out of Town

Falling, falling
until breath wanders out of itself, transforms and is lost
and then there is simply a disembodied pulsing
a small dark bird
a nub

Boats
with a single lamp ride the water's lip, and the quiet
keeps vigil for a small intrusion: the shadows
presage so many things
but no intrusion, only some memory unhoused

Variations on Half
of a Line by Mallarmè

Helas, the flesh is sad and money
old pianos of flesh sad
money and yeast
of voices
the steady buzz
no bell or shriek can tear
padded so no plumb no
nothing but sad old pianos
of flesh no money the yeast
of voices no refuge
but rain the rain
between night's eastern entry
and morning your flesh
half sun half clay
the chittering sparrows
your old sad piano
its eighty-eight strokes
and rain
our only covert no
spoor no money no place
our refuge
rain and flesh sad flesh

Song #1

No one said
jiggle stuck syllables till the sow
drops piglets

and we'll buy
you a cottage way back in the trees
with fat fat June bugs

that slap the screens
No one said
grub your noggin night

and day
and here's a stack of 78's
by the one the only

Memphis Minnie
Sing for your supper and look
what you get

potato eyes and a helium crepe
And for dessert, Monsieur?
Sincere best wishes

Put in another slug
and I'll tell you what else
No one said

Boo

Dejection Between Foot and Brow

Mr Moo heard stuff 'round the trough
ah me, dumb
like a yoke. Iz cumulative
you know
till the hole's plugged
and what it is backs up
to the doors of Penny Palace.
                                    The racket, man
in that arcade—those slobs
at toy war go *unh*, *unh* night and day.
                                    Remember
the world, Beau
2 miles high
so any chair or bough was bright
like the eye-fur
burnt off.
                Birds just shot through
the arch
screaming,
                Jeeeeezus, my feathers
my pretty little bones . . .
                                    I remember
where was that
in Troy, I think—
                        or some dry hill
out west.
It's years now.

Ahasuerus

There was no hazard so we left off
when night fell.
The wind spoke too slowly to fathom.
Voices, lights
drifted away from us like a cloud of gnats.

I can remember that first morning
when we woke athwart the world.
Even the light had its own strange scent.
Any sudden shadow of bird or branch
triggered a shock between our genitals and spine.

The worst, naturally, was the waiting.
Whisky, chess and sentences
that broke off
only to reconnect past memory's gate.
The gardener scything out there was wild himself.

When the girls arrived we swam to the point, fucked,
and walked back
along the gravel road to the highway.
The sun drew out the echoing in our blood
but by then we were already listening like tourists.

After a winter the villagers,
dull salacious eyes in tiny heads, warmed
to us, confided to us
their peculiar gossip and lore.
Their wives brought cookies.

We learned nothing.
The cookies tasted like rancid dust.
But when we looked in the mirror
we were both ourselves and otherwise.
Spirit and flesh played blithely in each other's yard.

The Luddite's Midnight Relapse

An orange, peakèd
to bad

wants out
of that lady's purse.

Now's the time
to make the grab

or she gets
off the bus and *eats* it.

Because I've got to
throw

that orange
quick

at any window on the block
still lit

or else
collapse into the shoe

business
muttering,   *Yeah*

*yeah   yeah
shoes*

*have their own little
tale*

of heartache and glee.
The moon

ought
never to break

the sea but
I . . .

From FDR Drive the Children
of Whitman Gaze Up

Lavender smoke from the Con Ed stacks
assembles its tufts
into bubbles of thought(viz., the funnies)high
               over the chilly river
and her bridges,
monuments of clunkish whimsy from an Age of Boom.

For the sky is synchronous this evening;
through the windshield its vistas
exactly right.
               Yes and speed too is sweet
at the golden hour,
dipping under viaducts and out
into heraldic light on the bounce

off Citicorp's roof,
the only pentahedron in sight,
up way up
               high for a street-rooted thing
but no kin of sky

as are those puffs wind
fails to scatter
but simply hang there like smudged zeppelins
one might be induced to
think scented
               while small craft higher yet
criss-cross
aimlessly over the factories and luncheonettes
of Queens
               clearly beyond this spectacle
and thou,
dreamily seeking your exit.

Song #2

There are among silences
favorite spots
which mix well with light
or like rock persist.
Name them; you name them not.

Go find yourself a serious weave
and storms are happy instruments.
I told this to my cat.
My cat derisively blinked.

Atoms never sleep;
that's how the juggler's balls
got beat.
          I'd rather speak of wine
than brick
or speak of nothing at all.

Invitation

Ah, but Anthea, these shallows
are for children and they are long asleep.
The lake, so black and still, beseeches us
with coolness to cut our bodies through.
The opposite bank is not too far
and what small creatures prowl below can but wonder
at that turbulence our legs and arms churn up.

Mosquitos will soon bleed us
pale as the moon, nowhere to be found, while lights
and music from the cabin above offer nothing,
less than nothing, retreat to our scabbards of fiction.

Come—
          our friends, friends by rote,
can puzzle to themselves
while we undress and swim far out
to the cool black eye of our histories.

The Tunnel of Love

In a place of trampled peanuts
ends the hunt.
     Dusk
brings on the lights and now
it is time for love.

But first a lemonade with ice
to startle
   the hot brain
and sweeten the tongue.

Down the ramp—
our prow slams through the door
and we are in night.
      Tickle my nose:
Aatchoo
    Gesundheit

How happy we are
with the flimsy horrors

alone

moving slowly.

Lines Written in Early Spring

Show elephants step through the 12th Avenue yards at
dawn
and a crocus sashed by a piece of pale blue cellophane
wins.
Hoy! sensible briefs flap over a hundred dim courtyards
and tonight, just as your molecule hotted-up goes nuts, so
mophrodites
will stream up subway steps again, heads bobbing this
way, that.

Pull down the screen, the wraparound screen of humming
phenomena:
bus honks, police sleeve piping and curbs.
See, more of the same, repainted, maybe a hydrant new,
but no pigment-wrung oblivion with mudras
flashing in space at the end of a girlish wrist.

Leave it for the great soul, the earnest and stentorian sap,
to airdrop pronouncements on warming tar roofs;
they're most of them harmless, just paying bills.
What's what is right at the tip of your nose
splitting cells to beat the band, taking no prisoners.

Sundown at Fletcher's Field

Ruder light was taken by sail
to the bishop of Seville
than this benison
suddenly on us like oil
pressed warm from olives.

The west goal mouth
is free for an instant but the kick
is high. Two wings
in green shorts cry out.

But the ball stays up. The sun
on its way down
has swallowed the world.
The park's suffused,

the shirts and the dogs,
with the burnish of Corelli's horns.

Show Business

                    That was a book I think you
were the Duchess
me the Stableboy
I remember now the horseapples
and itchy wool it was never that way
but God were you ever a Sireen
that I do remember and how the Townsfolk

flushed you'd have thought a gram
of niacin was in them instead of you
on your way out of the Butcher's
with half a roast and some mustard
under your arm turning suddenly
with that look of sexual malice I think
you were rich but I forget who

it was betrayed whom and were we
in love the Players most of them are
still in the Directory we could phone
and ask that is except your Sister
who perished poor thing the Actress
who took her part was gallant but missed
that delicacy of nature which killed

your Sister whom I do remember
but the rest what was between us
how the garden smelled the electric
storms were we or not I wonder
how we are punished for forgetting
or let go numb
somewhat more smooth charming and mean

Summer's End

Seven miles through tangled bush and on
to the HoHo outpost.
A steady trickle from spruce boughs above
has us telling thetruththetruth
to tree frogs and slugs.
Weariness, wet socks and a keen deltoid rheum
have turned the world back on us.
Flynn commences to whistle, inhale
and whistle, whistling nothing
but a thread of abuse
at the blameless cedar, or hoping
perhaps to flush a nervous eagle.
I think not.
And on:

> whittling maledictions
> two miles in an afternoon

on to the HoHo outpost.

No sooner had our people sung us
to the forest's edge
than the radio weevil was on them,
leeching the private knowledge.
As for the news ahead—
HoHo is in ruins
and the hamadryads far,   far.

Thus clenches the world
as the sibyl long ago told us it must
long ago under the weaving poplar.
Too far gone to turn around
we journey again for journey's sake.
Sick with woe?

> *HoHo,*
> Flynn shouts to the sun
> and the shout resounds

Semper HoHo!

Friday Morning in the Haight

The gray man at the door
of his rental t.v. shop pauses,
bent
with pain shooting through like the express

at a local stop. Gas
maybe
or cancer working the membranes.
A cloud of spider motes

swaddles his head,
evaporates.
The gallery of Zeniths in half-light
. . .

There's a real deal in back
for burn-outs, students and pensioners:
a black&white set,
1958.

Deep in its cool metal sheathing
a ghost constellation
traces itself among atoms—
half-blown neon in a snowstorm.

It is Perry Como,
velvet throated Italian barber,
and he is singing
                    Quando Quando Quando

through eternity.

Warm Night in February

It smells of summer out,
she said
      in Safeway's parking lot,
tilting her head
to reach more air.

There is a kind of wave
that falls upon us
unawares.
      I cannot tell you
how it comes or when
but we are left there broken,
our voices everywhere scattered.

Kid Clarinet

Let 'er go, say Colonel Jack

but once I got hold
I keep it

I keep it straight
I keep it sideways

Sideways then straight

Let 'er go, say Colonel Jack

but this be the Glory Turnpike
world fall in behind

Let 'er go, say Jack

But this be the sweet lane

    More I blow
        sweeter it get
    Harder I blow
        sweeter yet

Get off it, kid
elsewise you kill it

But I fall down blind and drown
a note so wild and wide

Let 'er go, say Colonel Jack

but he ain't been where I have

Christmas Eve on Haight Street

It's always the same guy with the Christ haircut
and jeans out at the knee
about to slide down the brick facing
between shops

dead or asleep. Two cops with mustaches
make note,
wisecrack about junkies and creeps
and radio the van.

Sky empurples over late shoppers
buzzing any larder,
the purple such a seller last year
and a favorite once for dying *acid.*

Fifteen years ago . . .

> *air buttery as May in Wichita*
> *boy Jesuses and melon-breasted girls*
> *heads asplash with purple*
> *dancing madly in the park nearby*

> *sky asplash with purple*
> *hand in hand a circle spinning*
> *late December tarantella*
> *children dancing till they fell*

> *Breughel bodies under a tie-dyed dome.*

Incident in Chinatown

Warmed by tea, sedate in a corner seat
I stare back at the cold afternoon,
its somber lintels, and continue to look
through the street's particulars: the red
pagoda on top of the phone booth,
trucks and wizened strollers.
Somehow the mind has gained a sail,
the sail a wind, and with this gift
the day breaks open and continues to open
until rubbish, tedium and gravities
vanish behind like an unregenerative port.
      Suddenly I'm clear, under a sky
bereft of signs, no course
but the course my wake describes.
So profuse are the apparitions—snippets
from rooms forgotten or never visited,
a bright Sunday photograph,
a sick great-aunt's perfume—
that the blood starts,
and something dark, deep down and dark
threatens to bloom into tearful exhaustion.
Then, just as suddenly, the wind gives out
and the waiter grins, impatient for my order.

An Autumnal Sketch

What to make of them, the professors
in their little cars,
the sensitive men paunchy with drink
parked at the fence
where the field begins and the suburb ends?

If there is a mallard in the reeds
they will take it.
They will take it and make it their own,
something both more than a duck
and less.

They so badly want a poem,
these cagey and disheartened men
at the edge of the field.
And before they turn back for supper
they shall have one.

Dispatch

Be still

Say nothing

Ask nothing of anyone

The ego is a ghost ship

Don't hurt your bones trying

This is only the end of a long day in June

The picnickers head home, feverish and drunk

Evening, in A-Minor

Methane is coming off them.
They pick at the rind
till worms find good jelly.
A muzz of voices, bonding—
a cloud, a caul, a cowl—
an atmosphere of sorts.
Wolf valence.

I know a pocket:
lily dust on the table,
cat in the fog.
               It's the world turned us out
before the membrane blew
and virus loose,
shards of toy biting anything pith.

A mutation, bless us,
till the sun undoes.
An isle—
plenty crayfish, lots bananas.
And . . .
      Segovia,
Segovia playing Fernando Sor.

Poetics

I have loved the air outside Shop-Rite Liquor
on summer evenings
better than the Marin hills at dusk
lavender and gold
stretching miles to the sea.

At the junction, up from the synagogue
a weeknight, necessarily
and with my father—
a sale on German beer.

Air full of living dust:
bus exhaust, air-borne grains of pizza crust
wounded crystals
appearing, disappearing
among streetlights and unsuccessful neon.

A CALENDAR
OF AIRS

Art & Youth

Pliny said these lights in the grass are stars;
a man walking home from his day's labor
needn't lift his head skyward to tell the signs.
Before the heavens were busy with Sputniks
and idiot beeps that say *hey!* to far off worlds
we ran at the lights with jars. We ran and ran
until nothing was left of our bodies to spend.

An ache so sweet was born those nights
in the heat, in the grass, at summer's waning
that we try for it years later in the dance
of lust and lust's passing.
                              Poor Swinburne,
dithery and gallant in great drafty rooms,
would have had this ache flogged back into him,
but the heart is soon corrupted
and love's accoutrements grow fierce.

Market

Out of the forests
and grasslands
           clutching
double-clutching
miles through industrial
meadows
        trucks
jolt
the arteries into town

hauling
tons of dead lamb
asparagus
and flounder miles

First come the women
in black
        cruising
the aisles

alert
for early zucchini
for lulas
and haddock
clear of eye

The daughters
-in-law
        shop later,
worthless
slatterns who miss
church
and know nothing.

Spleen

The night Ottawa brought down the budget
Mrs. Mooney's pals sat shit-faced in the bar
next to three Québecois, brilliantly scarved.
Around the block streetlamps intruded
on clusters of branch—
                              et voilà:
catkins dripping from ash.

A hundred million was spent to make jobs.
Bronchial trouble was in every house.
March had been wet. Dark women looked pale;
fair women, sallow. All that day
the skin doctor lanced eruptions.

Bankers were generally pleased.
The last traces of black snow became air
and that air trailed a slow Greyhound
to the Dairy Queen in Plattsburg.
It was a budget without surprises.
The dead were dead. The rest of us on call.

The Prodigal on Home Court

Crickets give me the willies
but mothballs are worse—
my sweatsocks will outlast me.
Home from points north,
west; years now
arriving by bus, plane, always
with useless books
and a sawbuck to my name.
My folks sleep. Older now
they shrug. A shrug means peace.
The stomach knows—
when the clams are bad or worse.
Fools place love in the heart,
but love is an acid
that laps the belly's walls.
The dirty aureole
across the Hudson is New York.
Jets sink into it. Here,
on the cliffs opposite,
trees whisk themselves.
The air freshens for rain.
Even George Washington, on the lam
from Howe, hid out here.
He ate and ran
south. Ask any Hackensack. Whisky's
the lad for tonight's ague.
Paddy's Nepenthe, for demigods
and skalds. These sheets
are Kerry blue,
so clean and cool
I could be afloat on a lake.

Ghosts

Ghosts
       loop-the-loop like mad.
     Impassive
to our little shames
they somersault all day.

Aether's their stuff; go
they must.
       Will,
even to the gunners
among them
        is less than air,
        less
even,
    than the shape
their noses
       carved
prow-like
       in their day. Relentless
as beavers
who chew or die
         they gambol
in our oats,
     buzz
       our marshdreams
move&move
      through
      and under us
who loved
    them
      helplessly
         in life.

Tell Me Whose Lips

Tell me whose lips
stop the biting thing, whose
touch is a drug.
The weeks pound on.

A dog loves whoever dishes
out the meat.
And a dog loves spring.

Those who vanquish the Fool-Killer
are safer than gold, than
bonds;
as sure as good land
in a shrinking world.

They thicken, accrue
(even as the thermostat
holds)
      just like robust mammals
do
when the weather turns

and grow another layer
when there is no air at all.

Lightning Bugs

A cruel word at eventide
and night zips up
like a spider's retreat.

Go back to your febrile
needlework.
         We shall not
be chasing lightning bugs
in the tall grass tonight.

Put the whisky on the shelf
and let us speak calmly
of money.

Nine Years After Bering

The merchant Tolstykh
found
in the Aleut of the Rats
great and high mountains
and low spots
between
covered with swamps
and also dry places
along the shore
where one may walk freely.
No trees
only driftwood; no
larch or poplars.
Sweet grass
from which brandy is distilled,
surpassing the sweet grass
of Kamchatka.
A burning mountain
to which islanders come
in skin boats
to take sulphur, bathe
in the boiling springs
or cook roots and sea meat
in plaited grass bags.
Men wearing wooden hats
of bent thin boards
glued
together with blood
from their noses.
Women with eagle and goose
feathers
behind their ears
and on their necks small
rounded stones
with painted seals' hair
and also white hair
of old people.

Parkas of sea parrot
over water
-proof shirts of sealion
belly.
That's it.
No shoes: summer   winter
moving
over rocky passes
barefoot.
Cut, they hold the wound
in hand
and let another sew it
shut
smiling the while
to evince valor.
When in winter
men go far out to sea
for halibut
and return senseless, unable
to walk
they take up 2 flint stones
birds' down
                    and sulphur
strike fire
and squat

until hot.
Of their amusements little
is known.
We do know this:
                    They have drums
and dance

with feathers in their hair

from **Big Foot**

Steps
sucking, glottal
Steps
along the line
of shore
black ice water
between his toes
hissing brine
in fur
One brief bolt
of light
in a fast sky
Not quite light
a vein of silver
in swimming rock
Steps
beat a measure
overtake the logy
pulse
Steps
making distance
Faint buzz
of a seaplane
behind boulders
of sky
is gone
by breathing sea
Steps

Dogs
peer from shrubs
and bolt
gargling delirium
at the ends of their leashes.
Dark rows of houses
with the incandescent box
in front parlors.
He does not knock.

The Inland Passage

Your sadnesses reign unbroken
as the north coast sky,
from the Charlottes up
the inland passage
where the weather stays hard;
a place the Tlingits fish,
a tribe almost bereft of art.
Bars open their doors at six
and fill up with white men,
bellies full of scrambled eggs,
chasing the grease with rye.

And when the weather breaks
in country like that, where
spring and autumn don't seem
to change a thing, a curious
distress comes to most faces
and the mountains, disrobed
of their mists, loom
above the town
with an unreal acuity.
It was on a day like that
I left.

Morning

Sun skims the brewery roof to no
    avail. To no avail it rides
the sooty ice—
        a worthless coin.

        We are up.
From two miles in space the frozen
    lake looks how . . .
chaste. Like an Alp? No
    big news below. Pontiacs
and snow. So many kitchens
    down there: the spacious
kitchens of Ontario, for instance.
    Out farm windows
acres that soothe the eye: billowed
    linen, a plate of thighs.
The river is only foolish
    in its turnings, foolish
in its turnings. The river
    is only foolish
in its turnings, nosing inland
    till it dies.

Boxing on Europe's Most Beautiful Beach

A slow breeze north from Africa
would not allow the surf to chill
our modest vinho, up
to its neck in sand, on time
to wash down heavy farm rolls
and oleaginating cheese-of-the-hills.

She surprised me, as bantam-weights
can do, with a neat left cross
to the side of the head
and thought to make a combination
with a straight right hand.

I ducked. At my back an igneous
bluff loomed burnt-sienna.
What was I to do? I counter-
punched, just above the elastic
waist of her skyblue underpants.
Down she went, doubled
like an embryo in sand.

Her arm raised to shield
her eyes from the winter sun
or me, was dark, the flesh mingling
nicely with the abundant strands
of down from her wrist to elbow.

Her breasts,
like troubled engines, rose
and fell as she worked to find
her breath. Her face, as soft
in line as any Burne-Jones painted
except for the gag-tooth
and chin, a trifle Slovak,
changed from a pellucid blue
to red to the kind of pink
uncommon but for the magnolia.
Reluctant to turn away,
though courtesy required it,
I brought the wine and rolls.
Is reciprocity not the kernel
of all Confucius taught? So when
she knocked the tendered cup
out of my hand, hope for perfect
accord spilt there too. And yet,
with unmistakable sweetness,
she did say,
                 Hit me again.

The Sausage-Master of Minsk

I was sausage-master of Minsk;
young girls brought parsley to my shop
and watched as I ground
coriander, garlic and calves' hearts.

At harvest time they'd come with sheaves:
hags in babushkas, girls plump
as quail, wrapped in bright tunics,
switching the flanks of oxen.
Each to the other, beast and woman,
goggle-eyed at the market's flow.

My art is that of my father:
even among stinking shepherds, bean-
brained as the flocks they tend, our
sausages are known. The old man
sits in back, ruined in his bones, a scold.

So it was my trade brought wealth.
My knuckles shone with lard, flecks
of summer savory clung to my palms.
My shop was pungent with spiced meat
and sweat: heat from my boiling pots,
my fretful labors with casings,
expertly stuffed. Fat women in shawls
muttered and swabbed their brows.
Kopeks made a racket on my tray.

But I would have none of marriage:
the eldest son, no boon,
even with the shop's renown, was
I to my parents. Among mothers
with daughters, full-bottomed, shy,
I was a figure of scorn.

In that season when trade was a blur,
always, from the countryside, there was one,
half-formed, whose eyes, unlike
the haggling matrons' squints, roamed
and sometimes found my own.
And of her I would inquire.
Before seed-time they always returned.

Tavern men speak freely of knives,
of this, of that. Call me a fool.
For in spring I would vanish
to the hills and in a week return,
drawn, remote, my hair mussed,
interlaced with fine, pubescent yarn.

A BL&T With Old Ed Hopper
at Gimbel's Luncheonette

She is not fetching
of manner or limb who draws near
in rayon, a dollop
of mayonnaise at her hem.
He of the explosive calves
will not mount her
in a squall of fond remarks.
Never. Always she will settle.
Dreamings will abandon her;
her girl's mouth too will
know the pinch of diminution.
Glum as a cow, Ed just chews
his pickle in a frame of bald
fluorescence. He does not smile
but he loves the pink swivel chair
and the doughnuts under glass.

Afternoon in the Middle Kingdom

Duststorms from the Gobi sack Peking.
The northwest suburbs vanish in a cloud.
Soon cheery bicyclists in thongs
sneeze up and down Great Boulevard,
falling headlong into ginkgos.
Cold sand wanders into hallways;
for weeks grit is found in spoon drawers,
in woolens, rose-petal jam and cats.
The French ambassador has a snit
about the joyless life. His wife,
whose perfume brings giggles at market,
once again tells her husband of Moon
Porcelain. But the city is gray
and vast, the parks in disrepair
and the sea three hours by rail.

Equinoctial Lines

My seventh autumn in the western mountains
and letters from the capital grow scarce.
At summer's end when the unearthly
blue of hydrangea was everywhere,
friends filtered down from the north
en route to new lives and old.
Already night had begun its encroachment
on the long, florid twilights of July;
curtains would be drawn before our guests
had finished their dinner wine; disquiet ensued,
polite smiles traded around the room.
Later, we walked down to the river.
It is always the same: my friends speak
broadly of life.   Once, the talk
was of lust, ambition. Now, disillusioned
by one or two lean winters, softer
in the belly, some of them balding,
they speak more of philosophy.
          What nights we have here in autumn
when the wind turns harsh and blows
to flame every light in heaven.
For days afterward I consider how far
along my friends have likely journeyed.
In a month all is forgotten. How strange
it seems whenever I am drunk in autumn
I can dream of nothing but life at the capital.

Superstitions

Trout bones are taboo to dogs.
If you catch a duck
put a feather through its nostrils.
If a woman eats fresh meat
it will make her nervous;
she might even die.
It is bad luck for young people
to eat greasy fish.
If a young person steps on blood
it will make him crazy.
A menstruating woman never walks
on the beach.
If a frog comes into your house
move.

High Tea in the Tropics

The moon on the bay is so big it's naughty.
How easily this smoke peels me down. Are these
integuments my psyche's scales or hooze?
That wind that just passed—how is it called?

    Only the eucalyptus breathings

I want a tuxedo. What I truly dream of
is rack upon rack of tuxedos
with nebulae on each lapel
and also of cummerbunds, indigo and gold.

Hey, I'm a pomegranate. Somebody kiss
me in a hurry or else I'll split.
You there, samba hips, and Black Betty, you
while we're in catapult range of heaven

        let's do the circle
        once slowly
        then dip

Vikings of the Air

Our skycraft rides too low to clear the heights—
Dump the goods, you scallywags, save this balloon.
The pink rocks of Arcadie fall out of sight;
down down through moving stacks of cloud
our plunder falls like defused bombs.
Peasant skulls explode in fields of chard.
The cargo we bartered bravely for is lost.
Screwed again. Heft brought us low
and close to jeopardy. Below, each spring
herring fishermen are likewise sunk by greed.
Happily, air is what fuels our craft
and we can buy air by dropping what we must.
Give them back what we fought like gods for.
Make height, you bastards. The wind
drives east toward the sea and our wives
are sure to moisten as our craft comes into sight.

POPPIES IN
THE WIND

Storm Over Hackensack

This angry bruise about to burst
on City Hall
will spend itself fast
so fluid and heat may build again.

But for a moment the light
downtown
         belongs someplace else,
not here
or any town close.

Look at the shoppers, how palpable
and bright
against gathering dark
like storied figures in stereoscope.

This is the gods' perpetual light:
    clarity
    jeopardy
        change.

Song #3

                Death for the quip
in a place with no bounce.
Ask nothing of the river wind
that could shake this heat.
                These blocks
of sorry, pitted brick
are instructive
          like tree rings, maybe
          or rot.

Elders on cafeteria stools
stir their Sanka,
                breaking
strange winds
that prophesy last things.

Gangster Jones' Analgesic
and Anti-Gravitational Device

You see, it's a total environment fits like a shoe.
What don't belong slips through
our *solar wind* feature just blows 'er out.
Not like those weeds crack cement and rune the conduit—
none of that.

So how do we know what don't belong?
(You're a regular philosopher, buddyboy.)
Because *you* programmed it, that's how.
And here's the beauty part:
you can forget or change your mind like a coked-up
                                        dolly on rollerskates

but this little baby won't.

Sunday Nocturne

Red pulse the big jet's lights
in descent.
          The aerial
on the plumber's duplex shakes.

Along these palisades the crowded
grids subside.
          Tonight

even lawyers
and hoods
approach the foothills of revery.

No pizza slice for the wayfarer
at this hour.
          Get thee to an inn, sport.

And still more jets,
dipping.
          From Dakar,
Akron and Samoa.
               A gentleman
in Italian loafers
disembarks.
Tomorrow at 1 he will bring
profound good news
to a steak joint in Moonachie.

Valentine Out of Season

Way back, little kumquat, bold petunia
mine. I say

way way back past the bleached cartoons
doilies and particles of moth

a world and a world again removed
from the ventilator hum

of the brain
avenging itself on the spinal cord

where the heat of the moon
is a pale red cloud on the amnesiac's brow—

From that far place I shiver and arrive
in you, my singular love

while even yet the lunging parts
of us splash and collide down the amazing flume

————————:

          she said. Past
          kindness,
unkindness
down came no hair. Thus
ends the tale.

          No meal of rant
          No billy-gruff jig
          No divots raked
              from the moonlit sod

The last light lit
is the magazine shop's

with its color photos of gash
        in baseball caps and knee socks.

Workout, With Nib

Incise
        the sheath of silky air,
        fuchsia, gold

The locus you don't want—
        break there
        or it breaks

Foetid, burning—
        after each angle worked,
        deal made . . .

Over you,
        flesh bubbling up
        like paint off a board

Très cher, trop cher—
        each beam shivering
        loose of its joint

Boy
        with a flame
        in a river of cicadas

That spot, there
        break it,
        there

Fat
        jumping in the sausage skin—
        burst it

Get in,
        pay the bill,
        get out

Canada Geese in New Jersey

                              Headed north
on the sodded-over trolley track
to Coytsville
              or until carbons blew free
of the brain-stem, out
both ears, settling like soot on wet grass

I heard a honk and made to duck
but two geese slanted past—
getting the hell out of here,
honking all night up the Hudson Valley.

Just like that: *honkhonk:*
a honk about as straight as their necks.
Two big geese can scare up the dead.
Then they're gone.

                              Azalea blossoms stir,
like so many tiny nightgowns.

A February Idyll

Groundhog stuck out his nose
wrong.
          Dumb hog, breathing
slow
in the half-light.
The gully's got you
good,
       got you so
the only place to go

is out,
with no key or carfare
home.
       Out, hog
and gone

to the studio lot
with chrome Daffy Duck
and Tokyo Rose.
          Brother,
you dead.

Shooting

The sun is high
and the blacktop soft so   *Hit*
first from the corner
then from the key
because your hand is hot
and no one's watching   *Hit*
and the sun's an oscilloscope
among ghostly ruins   *Hit*
and out jumps memory—
Cerberus!   *Hit*
nothing happens   *Hit*
your brow's sore from salt
mixed with poisons escaping   *Hit*
for forget-me-nots
sprinkling the tall grass   *Hit*
for the poppies for birdsong
pale nubs   *Hit*
so your flanks start to glisten
like fish do   *Hit*
and young mothers pull their shades down
Hit   get hit back
till you're ripe for a juicing
Hit   on a hill in the Peloponnesus
your limbs oiled and kneaded
your focus burned clear   *Hit*
after dark and the stars shall
illumine
Put moves on the locals
They'll make you a god

Hit   for the sake of it
for the music of hitting   *Hit*
because will ordained it
and you can deliver
Hit   you the Hit Man
Hit   'cause Jim Dandy's
got nothing on you   *Hit*
because you've been hitting since when
at the playgrounds   *Hit*   underneath
then hook with both wings
Hit   twice for compassion
and 3 times for passion   *Hit*
one more time
and all sins are absolved
Hit   for the rhythm
that finds you and lifts you
The ball is a planet
and you make it go

Trolley

The trolley runs out to the sea
swivels
     and comes back
under the sidewalk where Crazy Jack
lays hands on faithless aerial rats.
His head's on springs.

The sea is colored mercury.
The trolley swivels
          and comes back
past skinny sidewalk trees
where almost no one is
but the corner grocerman, his cupcakes
and linoleum.

The trolley runs out to the sea
swivels
     and comes back
'cross avenues that once were dunes
and crones now perch,
pelicans in chubby shoes.
They're waiting for the trolley

runs out to the sea
swivels
     and comes back
to crewcut Rituh,
she's a butch little teasuh
sheezuh

swivels
>and comes back
to MickeyMike
raking the grill with his spatula
He's got the Cuban beans
>authentic sauce
>whadayaneed
MickeyMike

>and comes back
to slick black kids with skinny hips
cow-eyed couples from far away
Chinese roots for a windy day
the mile-long circus where no one pays

and runs out to the sea.

The Interior Decorator on Sunday

Those strange and translucent scampi in lantern hats
who graze then vanish into night's big hole
are here, shorted-out, hard
to pick up in the neutral air,
but afloat between ceiling and carpet.
No, they are not. They are off
across the ravine of bison grass and dead shoots,
over the boulevard and gone
to spin or park on their filament's last inch.

On the wall is a spot: the painter sneezed
. . . or dirt,
or it is a cousin back from the dead
yearning to touch brows.
The spot is not monochrome; red is with that gray.
It is . . . a cell beset by virus.
Really, I don't know. So much business thins me out.
And now voices approach: they are spheres,
textured.

Good Sound at Lake Fork

I heard the dead lodgepole creak
just before dark and the heavy cold.
You enjoy a sound like that;
it's the news in a black cowboy hat
about to lay his shadow
between us and the golden hills.

Every night, after the barkers and dolls
quit work, swinging their lunchpails
down the block, we watch
as the day's set goes up in flames.
Some nights we toast marshmallows
and get sentimental,

ever the suckers for burning facades.

To a Friend

Let them tell you how the months will turn
away from our season,
how these little panics that bite
into days
          like some wicked saxophone
cease.

    But distance, silence
and these brutish fits of wind off the sea
distress the blood, ridicule
our spirits
         and bring us to unnatural fatigue.

Tenderloin: An Etymology

Electric here is closer to the skin.
Receptor hairs on top
tell anything,
givegivegiving the nerve.

                                         Thus, tender.

Loin is warm;
even at night it's warm. Sleep
with fists in there tight
if you're cold.

                              No hotel is too cold.

Loin is the hub,
its breathing ceaseless. Within
protein gathers unto its template,
pieces falling

                             that enzymes may burn.

And then the smell

Cautionary Lines for a Thriftless Lady

For what?
A basket of napless wool mice, granny junk.
Not much return on what was spent.

There is a bottom.
There is absolute bottom,
a notion.

Between the two, place and notion,
silt—
a null zone.

You get there by scratching
the length of you against bottom.
Scant notion in that.

You scratch till you get through.
To silt.

Nothing up against you then.
You fall.

Only.

Toward an idea.

Any idea.

Chrysalis

Some big rain in the night
washed away what I know.

The morning pavement is dry
but everything I recognize is gone,
was not so ever.

                That pitiful armature
I drape clothes on
was never there at all.
                Lighter
at both shoulders
I go.

Words bubble up and burst
at the gate to the world—
dead spores in an updraft.

Blessed be the gyro
that keeps us afloat
                who go on pumping

even as we toss

in the wild.

Song #4

Flora—

I write the name you never used

Damask&Camellia

garden cool with bands of shadow

Flora

Floralia

even the birds remember

acid   sweet

another spring sifts through

Staying Home From Work

That is a mower from the city
you hear in the park
so mild a day no heat
nowhere to be till lunch
nothing to think
money
nobody
lie still and listen
like the boy did
long ago
listening to neighbors mow
sniffing summer through the curtains

Such care the city takes
not to let grass grow
too long
and should you fall again
to dreaming
no one will reproach you
or come seek you out
to put you off this sweetness
so rare
so minor a key were it music
if fabric
would come apart in your hands

Ye Olden Barge

As Plot rounded the corner
ants got him,
twirling in his sugar and pith

took the ground out
from under him,
tunneling, putting down eggs

dismantled the protein church
within sight of Denouement—
no ride.

To get from here to there
in the grand curve,
every inch a storm of bites . . .

Poppies in the Wind

The honeybee
painting himself his delight inside her
the both of them
adrift
tossing in fits of wind
petals of her knees
raised up around him
petal arms
encircling in shadow his cameo'd frenzy
hosts of them
open or clenched
waving
sheathed or half out
of their witch-hats
at May's meridian
drying like chicks in the air

Wind and Pine

He kept to the pine
while the wind was up,
courting.
   Mists
came and went,
did this thing or that
with treeline   ocean
  ridge.
    Evening cloud
went through its paces:
charcoal copper
   textures shapes;
  transformation
scorning art.
    He climbed
onto the shape of sound
the pine gave off,
     slid
and fell back,
nothing in hand

  wind through pine

music
grabbed for
   vanishing
swift
as the two startled bucks
met
  by our scent.

Hollyhocks in the Fog

Every evening smoke blows in from the sea,
vapor of lost destroyers.
It hangs over the eucalyptus grove,
blocks every height,
curls around garbage sacks
next to a lesbian bar.
A black dog takes a long sprint through it, stops
squats and runs on.
               Cold smoke
seeps into the bloodstream, cancelling
the high ground of memory and pain—
a kind of war drug.

Some small piece is lost each time the smoke
moves through.
There is a part will have slipped away
when the sun burns back the world.
Here is a specific chill we wrap
ourselves against nightly.

Only the hollyhocks contend anything,
indelible and bright—
beacons, trembling.
What are those? I asked a friend
my first summer.

Now I wait for them.